THE KERNEL

LIFE-CHANGING PRINCIPLES FROM THE POWER OF ANTS

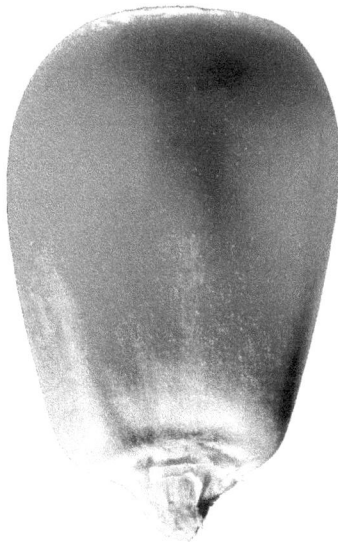

James M. Morrison & Andrew J. Siddoway
With Curt B. Dahl

www.OptioInstitute.com

Printed in the United States of America

Illustrations by: Matthew Quayle

The Kernel:
James M. Morrison; Andrew J. Siddoway; Curt B. Dahl - 1st ed.

ISBN: 978-0-9839434-3-3

10 9 8 7 6 5 4 3 2 1
First Edition

Table of Contents

The Beginning

He sat motionless wondering how something so small could capture his complete attention. He, the most powerful man on earth, fascinated by ... an ant?!

Timor the Great, 14th Century conqueror of Persia and most of India and Asia, founder of the Timurid dynasty, and world's most feared warrior now sits alone, defeated - hiding from his enemy in an empty abandoned stone building.

Slowly, the sting of his recent defeat is dulled as the "Lord of the Sun," focuses on a single ant crawling next to his sandaled feet. But it's not the ant that first captures this conqueror's attention. It is a single kernel of corn the ant is moving. Watching intently, the world's greatest ruler becomes the world's most humble student.

Timor watches with interest as the ant pushes this kernel towards a small wall. He's impressed with the strength the ant possesses in pushing this large kernel, but he also sympathizes that the ant's struggle will be in vain. Even this courageous insect will never have the strength to lift the kernel of corn over the wall. It's impossible.

Timor's thoughts are carried away to the battlefield, his army, and his conquered lands until he again notices the ant. Undeterred by the weight and overpowering size of the kernel the ant struggles to lift the needed food over the wall.

Certainly, he reasons, the ant will die from exhaustion before it can lift this kernel over the barrier. After all, the weight of the kernel itself is many times greater than that of this foolish ant.

To pass the time, Timor begins counting the ant's attempts at lifting the kernel over the wall.

After the first five failed attempts, a pursed smile favors his lips. Ten, and then twenty failures bring a shake of his head at such stupidity. The thirtieth, fortieth, and then sixtieth attempts all bring the same futile result. Only Timor's boredom and curiosity stop him from lifting the kernel so the ant can continue its path homeward to be welcomed as an abundant provider.

Timor's count is now at seventy. Again, the ant starts its task, this time using everything it has learned and all the strength it possesses. Slowly the small ant lifts the massive kernel up further, further, further than ever before, and finally... over the top of the wall.

The mighty Timor the Great, the most powerful and feared warrior in the world, gazes in awe at the accomplishment of this single ant. Timor didn't conquer the world without learning valuable lessons along the way, but this day, he learned from an ant the most important of all,

– stick to it and never give up.

A mighty and majestic man walks away from the abandoned stone building with renewed strength and determination to change his world. With this lesson indelibly impressed on his inner soul, Timor rises gallantly from defeat.

Seven centuries later the lessons learned by the world's most powerful warrior from a single ant inspires survival and success in our own complex world. But what was learned from this ant so long ago is only the beginning of what it can teach us today.

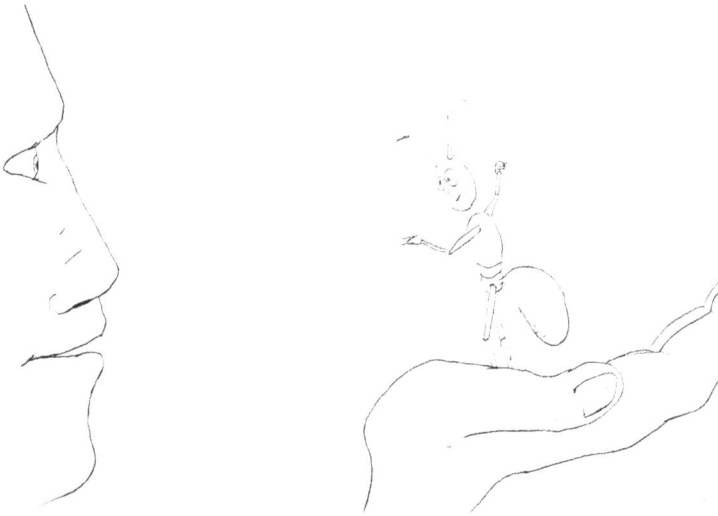

The Ant

From the 14th Century fast-forward nearly 700 years …

He stared motionless wondering how something so small could capture his complete attention. He, the most powerful man in his *corporation,* fascinated by… an ant?!

Out on the rolling landscape for a solitary early morning run this icon of the business world slows his pace to a standstill, places his hands on his knees, catches his breath, and takes in the tranquil scene. He is awed with the peacefulness of the moment. The birds sing in the background and a gentle breeze blows through a nearby tree. But unexpectedly none of these miracles of nature catch his attention.

His full gaze focuses on an anthill at his feet. He watches with interest. The ants all scurry about in organized chaos. He smiles to himself thinking how absurd their lack of purpose seems. Certainly, he thinks smugly, such an organization would never last in his complex corporate world.

He exhales one final deep breath preparing for the upcoming miles and he hears something unique – a faint, "Hey!" His head whips around to see who is near him. Looking around he sees no one. Again he hears a distant, "Hey!"

Where is this coming from? There is no one within 5 miles of him right now. "Hey!" It seems like it's coming from near his well-worn running shoes. He looks closer. And then closer … this isn't happening … is it?

BBA, MBA, JD, CFO, CEO. He has enough letters behind his name to start his own alphabet. Someone of his intelligence can't be hearing an ant standing next to his feet speaking to him. He feels absolutely foolish getting on his knees and taking a closer look.

"Yes, you. I'm talking to you," the Ant shouts.

This must be a mean trick. If so, a man of his learning, experience, and savvy is going to get to the bottom of this.

The Beginning

His face is now within inches of the ant who has separated from the rest of the colony. The voice is now clear.

"Are you going to talk to me or just let me continue with a monologue?"

Sheepishly and uncertain what to say, the mighty business executive replies, "You're talking to me?"

"I don't see anyone else around here who speaks human, do you?" The Ant isn't waiting for any reply. He's got an audience and he's going to use it.

"I know what you're thinking," says the Ant.

"That an ant talks?" Replies the executive.

"Of course not" the Ant quickly retorts. "You're thinking that my ant colony, my little company, couldn't make it in your high powered world."

"How do you know that?"

"Look, if an ant is talking to you, can't you also believe I know what you are thinking," the Ant says boastfully.

A million thoughts flood the business executives mind. Is it providence, intuition, or just dumb luck that has brought him to this anthill?

"Call it opportunity," the Ant proudly announces. "Because you are wrong about the efficiency of my community. For one thing this place is filled with workers. Do you know how many people work for your company, Mr. Big Shot?"

The Executive thinks and is about to answer when the Ant interrupts him. "I know, about half of them."

The Ant rolls on his back and kicks his six legs in laughter at his quick wit. "About half of them … get it?" Rolling back on his feet he gets serious. "You see, in my colony everyone has a job and we are all very good at what we do. We all work and we all work hard. Without strong workers we would not survive, and guess what? This isn't something we learned last night! It's only taken us MILLIONS of years to get the organization we have today. Remind me again how long you've had your structure? I know," the Ant says not waiting for the executive's reply, "since your last *restructure* two years ago. Boy, do you have a lot to learn."

The Ant continues in non-stop banter. "I've seen your organizations. Silos … everyone trying to build kingdoms. You call that effective? You have politics, in fighting, and power mongers. We have workers. Purposeful workers. Effective workers. Fulfilled workers."

"And our workers may have one or several jobs we do well and with precision. We switch tasks as needed. We may keep the same job all our lives or occasionally change jobs. Some of us gather. We find and gather our food. Others store the food, and others dig the tunnels and build the chambers. We also have workers who defend our community from what you might call, hostile takeovers. And does it work, I see you thinking?"

The executive furrows his brow knowing this is exactly what he is thinking.

The Ant continues in rapid conversation. "Of course it works and it's worked for how long?"

"Millions of years," whispers the Executive.

"Louder, please," the Ant shoots back.

"Okay, millions of years," the executive speaks loudly.

"Then don't you think you can learn a lesson or two from we simple ants that will help you achieve greatness in your company and in your life?"

"Okay, I'm all ears," the Businessman begrudgingly admits as he sits on the ground next to the ant.

For the next several minutes, much like Timor the Great, from the 14th Century, the renowned business executive is about to become the humble student of an ant.

Universal Principles

"Now, you're pretty successful, right," the Ant says, complimenting his student.

"Most people say that," the Businessman freely admits.

"You're a big deal in your world – a mover and a shaker – a get it done kind of guy," the Ant strokes the ego of his pupil. "Why are you so successful?"

"I work hard and see that those working with me work hard, too," replies the Ant's star pupil.

"I see." The Ant ponders this response while resting his large head upon his folded front legs. "You work hard."

"That's the secret," the Businessman says with pride.

"Well, I have news for you. That isn't a secret and it isn't the secret of your success," the Ant retorts. "If you think working hard is the secret to success then the slaves who built the pyramids in Egypt should be the most successful businessmen in the history of the world, but they aren't. Now, I'm going to share with you a nugget of 'Ant Wisdom.' Listen closely and you'll have greater success, both in your business and in your personal life … and it isn't about working harder. It's starts with universal principles."

"Universal Principles," the Businessman asks? "Like science?"

"Call it what you will," the Ant continues, "but the first key to greatness is recognizing and respecting universal principles in your situation."

"My ant colony is a perfect example of how timeless and universal principles are the foundation for everything we do. After all, we've spent how long …?"

"Millions of years," replies the Businessman in rote fashion.

"Right. Millions of years getting it correct," the Ant smiles.

"Universal principles operate regardless of how we feel about them and when rules are violated, predictable consequences follow. See that field over there," the Ant points with his spindly leg? "What universal principle does the farmer align himself with before he considers planting?"

"I'm not exactly sure. I'm no farmer, but I imagine it's important to plant the field at the right time," the Businessman surmises.

"Ladies and Gentlemen, we have ourselves a winner," the Ant congratulates the Businessman. "It has to be done at the right time. He can't change it. There is a time to prepare the soil and a time to plant. Everything being done in order or it will not work. Now what other universal principle does the farmer consider?"

The Businessman gives a clueless shrug.

"Well, it's a good thing you're not a farmer," chides the Ant. "He needs to give the plant time to grow, mature, and ripen. You see his corn over there," the Ant points? "Well after a corn "silks" it normally takes about 55 to 60 days for it to mature. If you try to pick it before then, you don't get a full harvest. Every farmer knows the law of the harvest is a universal principle that can't be ignored. These universal principles must be understood for organizations and individuals to have success like our colonies."

"Now," the Ant continues, "What are the universal principles of your life? What are the universal principles of your business? What are your universal principles of greatness?"

The Businessman can't believe it. He has no answer.

"Until you know the universal principles in your life, you will never reach the greatness you desire. I'll say that again," the Ant states with authority, "Until you know the universal principles in your life, you will never reach the greatness you desire. So start thinking about it. We won't go any further until you determine your principles. But here are a few examples that will help you.

Honesty, Integrity, Balance, Persistence, Understanding, Communication, Profitability, etc.

The Kernel Journal - *Universal Principles*

How would you define greatness in your life?

_____

_____

_____

_____

_____

_____

_____

_____

What are the universal principles to help you achieve greatness?

_____

_____

_____

_____

_____

_____

_____

_____

The Kernel Journal - *Universal Principles*

Who is essential to your achieving greatness and why?

_____ — _____
_____
_____

_____ — _____
_____
_____

_____ — _____
_____
_____

_____ — _____
_____
_____

_____ — _____
_____
_____

_____ — _____
_____
_____

Common Purpose

"See my co-workers running about over there," the Ant asks the Businessman? "What do you see?"

"Chaos," is the Businessman's quick comeback.

"Your chaos is my common purpose," the Ant surmises. "Do you really believe that after millions of years of evolving and developing we have any wasted motion or unproductive efforts?"

"I know ... Millions of years," the Businessman shakes his head.

"If we adapted our work to look like yours, guess what?" The Ant continues not waiting for an answer. "We'd be extinct and you wouldn't have anyone letting you in on the secrets to greatness. So listen up."

"I'm all ears," the Businessman concedes.

"I've noticed their incredibly large," nods the Ant with a smile in his voice. "What you call chaos we call 'Common Purpose.'"

"You have common purpose," the Businessman asks with perplexity?

"Of course we do. The fact that you can't see it is evidence of our efficiency," the Ant proudly proclaims. "We changed, evolved and, how do you say it, 're-structured' for nearly 86 million years to come up with the perfect organization. It's been so effective that we haven't had to change it in over 6 MILLION years. When was your last 'restructure?' Oh, never mind I really don't want to embarrass you in front of my friends. With our common purpose every one of us knows who we are, what role we play, where our contribution fits, why our job is important, and how others depend upon our skills. Knowing these important things makes all the difference. That's one of the flaws in your organization. Not everyone knows the answers to these simple questions."

"What are the questions, again," the Businessman asks?

"Who, What, Where, Why, and How," the Ant replies rubbing his tiny legs on the temples of his large head. "Who you are? What role you play? Where your contribution fits? Why your job is important, and how your fellow workers depend on your skills? It's the foundation for common purpose. If your workers can't answer these questions, you won't bond with common purpose. Eighty-six million years taught us this lesson and I've given it to you in 5 minutes. It's common purpose that is motivating me today just as it was motivating my ancestor hundreds of years ago to try SEVENTY times to move a kernel over a wall. Common purpose gives us this kind of tenacity and work ethic. Is there anyone in your company beside yourself who will show this dedication?

The Businessman purses his lips and sadly shakes his head.

"Who, what, where, why, and how," the Ant reminds him. "Answer these questions and you'll have people doing extraordinary things and discovering greatness. It's all about discovering your common purpose and common purpose leads to greatness."

The Kernel Journal - *Common Purpose*

What is your purpose?

_____

_____

_____

_____

_____

_____

_____

_____

Why is this your purpose?

_____

_____

_____

_____

_____

_____

_____

_____

The Kernel Journal - *Common Purpose*

How will you fulfill your purpose?

_____

_____

_____

_____

_____

_____

_____

_____

_____

_____

_____

_____

_____

_____

_____

_____

_____

_____

Accountability

"Have you noticed our foreman over there," the Ant inquires of the Businessman?

"Don't tell me, let me guess which one he is," the Businessman responds as he peers over the ants. "Is it that one," he points at a larger ant?

"Trick question," laughs the Ant. "We don't have a foreman. We have a Queen who oversees us. There's no foreman, no boss, no supervisor telling us what to do or how to do it. Our actions are simply manifestations of what lies deep within us. You know the things that can't be measured, like dedication, understanding, commitment, … we believe so deeply in our common purpose and in our shared goals that we aren't told what to do or how to do it … it's just part of us. Now, how much will you pay for an employee like that?"

"I don't know," the Businessman thinks, "I don't have anyone like that."

"The accountability that lies in each is what drives us. If you want greatness in your company, you need greatness in your employees and trust me, millions of years has proved that greatness comes from within. You can't force internal accountability on anyone, man nor ant. Oh, you can force them to do things, but as soon as you stop pushing they stop, too. Force never leads to greatness. You can have efficiency – You can have competence – You can have even have some success, but you will never force greatness. Greatness comes from individual accountability and this comes from within. Start with universal principles and common purpose and it's much easier for us to find individual accountability," expounds the Ant.

"Interesting concept," nods the Businessman.

"Concept?!! A concept is something that isn't proven. We prove the worth of Individual Accountability with … remind me again," urges the Ant.

The Businessman nods, "Millions of years of practice."

"Well said," the Ant smiles.

The Kernel Journal - *Accountability*

How strong is your personal accountability?

_____

_____

_____

_____

_____

_____

_____

_____

How strong is your professional accountability?

_____

_____

_____

_____

_____

_____

_____

_____

The Kernel Journal - *Accountability*

How will you improve your weak points?

_____

_____

_____

_____

_____

_____

_____

_____

_____

_____

_____

_____

_____

_____

_____

_____

_____

_____

_____

Teamwork

"Do you see any of us doing exactly the same thing over there," the Ant asks the Businessman?

"Well, it doesn't look like it," is the Businessman's reply.

"So everyone's doing their own thing," queries the Ant?

"Pretty much I'll say. But I have the feeling

you're telling me otherwise," says the Businessman knowing he probably isn't seeing the obvious.

"This is the perfect example of teamwork," boasts the Ant.

"Please explain," shrugs the Businessman.

"When you're watching a basketball game, what do you see," inquires the Ant?

"Five tall guys running around in shorts and shirts putting a ball in a hoop," is the Businessman's answer.

"Do they all have to be tall," asks the Ant?

"Well, I guess not," is the Businessman's answer.

"Exactly. There may be many tall players crowding around the basket, but the ones dribbling the ball up the court are often no bigger than you," says the Ant, tapping on the Businessman's chest with his little leg. "Put the tallest player next to the shortest player, put them in street clothes and ask anyone what these two have in common and the last thing you'll hear is, 'They are both basketball players.' They look nothing alike. But if your team only has tall players who can jump or only short players who handle the ball, you have a team that is lacking some very important positions. Our different roles in the colony give us strength as a community. Our collective contribution is exponentially greater than our individual effort. Using individual strengths and working together for the betterment of our colony is why we have success. We know well defined and different skills are another ingredient to greatness."

"It's hard to argue with millions of years of success," the Businessman determines.

"You are catching on," smiles the Ant.

The Kernel Journal - *Teamwork*

What do you value in others?

_____

_____

_____

_____

_____

_____

_____

_____

_____

_____

_____

_____

_____

_____

_____

_____

_____

_____

The Kernel Journal - *Teamwork*

What keeps you from partnering with others?

_____

_____

_____

_____

_____

_____

_____

_____

_____

_____

_____

_____

_____

_____

_____

_____

_____

_____

Diversity

"Are you married?"

The Businessman turns the wedding ring on his finger. "Happily married. Why do you ask?"

"And is the secret to your happiness rooted in being exactly alike," the Ant sarcastically asks?

"Well, I thought we were a lot a like when we got married, now I think we're total opposites," admits the Businessman. "But we love each other more than ever."

"And her strengths make up for your weaknesses and your strengths help her weaknesses," comes the sage insight of the Ant.

"Absolutely," agrees the Businessman.

"This is another lesson in finding greatness," expounds the Ant. "Diversity is strength. Filling a company, a social circle, or even a marriage with people who are exactly the same slows growth and accomplishment for everyone. Do you know there are nearly 12,000 species of ants with various levels of diversity from colors, shapes, and lifestyles? Our development teaches us diversity is essential to longevity. Diversity of thought and opinion is healthy."

"Entertaining conflicting opinions is like riding a roller coaster," sighs the Businessman.

"True," replies the Ant, "But I always have a better time riding a roller coaster than I do sitting on a merry-go-round. The merry-go-round just makes me dizzy; the excitement of the roller coaster brings me energy and drive. Just as I prefer the elation of a roller coaster, greatness prefers the exhilaration of diversity."

The Kernel Journal - *Diversity*

What is the value of diversity?

_____
_____
_____
_____
_____
_____
_____
_____

What can you learn from other people, cultures, and generations?

_____
_____
_____
_____
_____
_____
_____
_____

The Kernel Journal - *Diversity*

What are the strengths in others that you would like to possess?

_____

_____

_____

_____

_____

_____

_____

_____

_____

_____

_____

_____

_____

_____

_____

_____

_____

_____

_____

_____

_____

_____

_____

Collaboration

""Silos," says the Ant.

"Silos," replies the Businessman?

"How do you feel about the silos in your corporation," the Ant inquires?

"Well, I'm told they hurt productivity," the Businessman slowly shakes his head.

"Not only productivity, but culture, execution, and strategy, as well," the Ant shoots back.

"To be honest, I have a hard time defining or even recognizing silos," admits the humbled Businessman.

"Look at my colony. What do you see in regards to silos," queries the Ant?

The Businessman looks at the ant colony for a moment and responds, "I certainly don't see any silos."

"Millions of years of reaching perfection teach us that silos ruin everything important in our colony. A cross section of our colony beneath the ground shows hundreds and sometimes thousands of interconnected passageways allowing us the opportunity of moving about to anyplace in the community. This way we all contribute and are not 'marginalized' by sitting forlorn in a silo," teaches the Ant.

"Imagine my colony in silos. One entrance for each silo. Time teaches us that silos thwart everything constructive and beneficial to our society. The independent and egocentric mentality of your world refuses to consider the impact individual decisions are having on other departments."

"Learning this lesson is learning to be an effective leader: Recognizing and eliminating silos as quickly as they form leads to undeterred progress."

"Just one more comment about silos," promises the Ant.

"Okay," the Businessman answers with relief.

"I believe," continues the Ant, "eliminating silos in business only comes after removing silos in your personal life."

"Just what I'm hoping for," complains the Businessman, "more difficulty in my life."

"On the contrary," states the Ant. "I admit losing silos in your own life isn't easy, but once these silos are removed recognizing silos and eliminating them in business is far, far easier."

"You see, it's all boiling down to collaboration. Your unique individual physical, emotional, spiritual, and mental abilities are all magnified when they gather together, just as they are minimized if separated into silos."

"One of your own says it well. 'The master in the art of living makes little distinction between his work and his play, his labor and his leisure, his mind and his body, his information and his recreation, his love and his religion. He hardly knows which is which. He simply pursues his vision of excellence at whatever he does, leaving others to decide whether his working or playing. To him he's always doing both." (James A. Michener)

"Mastering the collaboration in your own self brings clear recognition, leading to the elimination of the silos that surround businesses and other facets of life. If we ants aren't practicing collaboration in every part of life, we are extinct. It's a lesson every ant learns for survival and it's an essential lesson in greatness."

The Kernel Journal - *Collaboration*

What are the behaviors of great collaboration?

_____

_____

_____

_____

_____

_____

_____

_____

_____

What do you need to do differently to better partner with others?

_____

_____

_____

_____

_____

_____

_____

_____

_____

The Kernel Journal - *Collaboration*

What do you need to do more of?

_____
_____
_____
_____
_____
_____
_____
_____

What do you need to do less of?

_____
_____
_____
_____
_____
_____
_____
_____

Loyalty

"In the Japanese language, the word 'ant' is created by linking two characters: one meaning 'insect,' and the other 'loyalty.' I am very proud we are defined as the 'loyal insect' by these wise people," proclaims the small Ant.

"Humbly stated, but greatly refined over the eons of time, we are loyal to one another. We rescue each other when injured; we stand side-by-side when facing difficulty. Where, my friend, is your loyalty manifest," the Ant asks sincerely?

"I don't know if this question has ever been raised or considered in my circles," admits the Businessman.

"Precisely the challenge for successful companies, and individuals," expounds the Ant. "Most don't think about it. This demonstrates a lack of understanding of what builds solid and sustainable unity in both organizations and in individuals."

"Loyalty is all about motivation," explains the Ant.

"My employees are motivated by their paychecks," proclaims the Businessman.

"Ah, yes, 'reward'," answers the Ant.

"Isn't that the number one motivator," suggests the Businessman?

"Most corporations and individuals think reward is best at motivating others," retorts the Ant.

"But in four categories of motivation 'reward' is second from the bottom. It only leads 'fear' in motivation."

"I know many who are totally motivated by the fear of losing their job," the Businessman recalls.

"I'm not saying," says the Ant, "that fear and reward don't motivate, I'm saying long lasting and meaningful motivation leading to sincere loyalty is based on something else, something more profound."

"Greater than fear and reward," asks the Businessman?

"Oh," responds the Ant, "so much greater and more effective."

"I'm ready for my lesson," the Businessman says settling in for a profound answer.

"The second highest motivator is 'duty.' Duty motivates from within. It's a strong attribute of loyal people. But 'duty' pales to the highest motivator which brings the greatest loyalty."

"What is it," the Businessman pleads?

"The answer is 'love,'" the Ant confidently states.

"I can understand how love builds loyalty, but is there a place for love in the business world," asks the Businessman.

"I'll answer the question with a question: Is there a place for love in the world?" Asks the Ant rhetorically.

"Of course," the Businessman dismisses the question.

"Then there is also a place for it in your business. Love builds loyalty. Ant's love what they do. They love being together. They love the success they achieve together. They love the way they are involved in the success of the colony. This love builds loyalty nothing else can possibly match," preaches the Ant.

"Love is the standard for success. People will do things out of love that they would never do for any other reason. This is the model for loyalty that money won't buy."

"In life, love fulfills. You are only fulfilled in your work if you are fulfilled in your life. Start there then spread this fulfillment to the workplace. Perhaps soon the Japanese will be linking your name with 'love' to symbolize 'Loyalty.'"

The Kernel Journal - *Loyalty*

How do you demonstrate loyalty?

_____

_____

_____

_____

_____

_____

_____

_____

_____

_____

_____

_____

_____

_____

_____

_____

_____

_____

_____

_____

_____

The Kernel Journal - *Loyalty*

How strong is your loyalty to those in your personal life?

_____
_____
_____
_____
_____
_____
_____
_____

How strong is your loyalty to those in your professional life?

_____
_____
_____
_____
_____
_____
_____
_____

Set Standards

"Great leaders set standards," the Ant next teaches the Businessman.

"Fair enough," the Businessman agrees.

"In our colony sharing roles is important, but no more important than working to a high standard. We hunt, gather food, protect each other, construct, and participate in building our colony. But if hunting or gathering only feeds a few, if constructing only houses most, and if protecting only brings security to some, we are doomed as a colony. Our standard is set. Every member knows the standard. Every member meets the standard. This is law in the colony. Consequences follow when standards are not reached."

"What type of consequences," the Businessman wonders out loud?

"The only consequences found in our society... natural consequences which are swift and brutal," says the Ant solemnly.

"So you are all well disciplined," the Businessman says making a mental note.

"Yes we are. But, I'm sorry your society thinks discipline is punishment or retribution. Do you know the root of the word discipline," ask the Ant?

"Do tell, oh wise one," bows the Businessman to his teacher.

"The root of discipline is disciple. See the difference between punishment and internal desire of following a standard," suggests the Ant? "We honor self-discipline as it develops hard work, persistence, creative thinking, character, selflessness, and self-control. The standards set and reached through self-discipline bring greater prosperity to the colony. Never forget setting and reaching standards; building on discipline and discipleship; these are the ways individuals and organizations reach greatness."

The Kernel Journal - *Set Standards*

What are your personal set standards?

_____

_____

_____

_____

_____

_____

_____

_____

_____

What are your professional set standards?

_____

_____

_____

_____

_____

_____

_____

_____

_____

The Kernel Journal - *Set Standards*

What are the natural consequences from not living the standards?

_____

_____

_____

_____

_____

_____

_____

_____

_____

_____

_____

_____

_____

_____

_____

_____

_____

_____

_____

_____

_____

_____

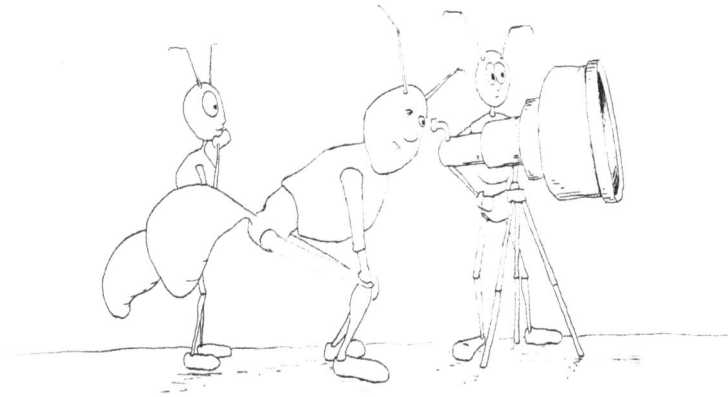

Vision

"Next," states the Ant, "is vision."

"Oh, how ironic," laughs the Businessman. "An ant telling me about the importance of vision. In case you aren't remembering correctly, ant's don't see very well. You work mainly by sense of smell."

"By your finite definition of vision," scolds the ant, "neither Helen Keller, nor Stevie Wonder, nor others posses the gift of vision."

"You have a point," mumbles the Businessman.

"Vision, like all other traits of greatness comes from within," admonishes the Ant. "And having no vision in your personal life renders vision in business as empty as a mirage."

"And what vision does the lowliest of ants possibly have," queries the Businessman?

"Every bit as much vision as the Queen. If not, there is no point in being part of our colony. Vision gives purpose. Vision gives meaning. Vision gives reason. One wiser than I once said, 'Where there is no vision, the people perish.' Certainly we know the importance of vision having survived millions of years," passionately exclaims the Ant.

"I notice in your culture vision is seen as an event. How wrong this is. Vision is a verb. It is actionable. It is ongoing diligence. It is continual motion. Just as a farmer looks at an apple seed and envisions an apple, he also knows his seed needs fertile ground. It needs ample water. It needs sunshine. It needs time. It needs cultivation and when completely grown, harvesting. Only then will he hold in his hand an apple. Only then is vision realized. You see, this is the power of vision. It's the power to bring about greatness."

"Vision represents faith. It represents hope. It represents belief. It is the motivation behind action. Vision replaces top down pressure with inner motivation. Vision allows belief in something bigger than the individual. Vision is critical to success. Without vision, work is a task. With vision, work is a cause."

"And making work a cause brings these essential principles of greatness together into each individual, and when it is in every individual it becomes a culture," exclaims the Businessman!

"You are beginning to understand," affirms the Ant. "Once within the individual, vision is permanently within the organization."

The Ant now pauses bringing importance to his next thought. "Consider this lesson above all else, 'Vision is the foundation of greatness upon which all other principles are built.'"

The Kernel Journal - *Vision*

What do you hope to accomplish in your personal life?

_____

_____

_____

_____

_____

_____

_____

_____

_____

What do you hope to accomplish in your professional life?

_____

_____

_____

_____

_____

_____

_____

_____

_____

The Kernel Journal - *Vision*

What will be the impact in your personal life?

_____
_____
_____
_____
_____
_____
_____
_____

What will be the impact in your professional life?

_____
_____
_____
_____
_____
_____
_____
_____

Attitude

"When you have vision, what kind of attitude does your culture have," the Ant asks the Businessman?

"A positive attitude," the Businessman responds. "But in my world, it's more about the result. We care little about the attitude if the business is productive."

"Is this true with your personal relationships,

such as your relationship with your friends and family," asks the puzzled Ant?

"No, of course not," the Businessman corrects the Ant. "I'm only talking business."

"This is a problem," the Ant shakes his head. "Why are you separating your personal situations and your business situations?"

"Because they are different," announces the Businessman.

"Here is an important lesson for you as you seek greatness. Your attitude is a constant. You don't suddenly change your attitude within the situation you find yourself. Positive attitude comes from within. In my world it permeates everything we are involved in."

"Look at our colony," the Ant instructs. "We are the most positive thinking species on the planet. We have a 'can do' attitude, which is a powerful influence throughout the entire colony."

"And I assume you're telling me this trait is imperative for success," the Businessman concludes.

"Not just success," exclaims the Ant. "It's essential for our very survival. Look at my fellow associates. We have within our colony a positive attitude bringing with it these attributes:

Satisfaction in our work
Contentment in our duties
Happiness in our activities
Fulfillment in our responsibilities
Joy in our relationships
Peace in ourselves and in others

"We are here to succeed as a colony and not to fail. Each ant in the colony knows attitude is a powerful trait that is individually owned. Positive attitudes that come from within are not swayed by outside opinions. We each know we have the ability and responsibility of our attitudes. These attitudes are who we are. They are not turned on and off depending on which function or role we are in. In the millions of years of adapting, I'm certain there were colonies where the attitudes of the workers were not positive or were changed depending on their circumstance. But here is another lesson. None of those colonies survived! Our success and survival is perpetuated because we have positive attitudes in everything we do."

The Kernel Journal - *Attitude*

How would people describe your attitude?

_____

_____

_____

_____

_____

_____

_____

_____

What controls your attitude?

_____

_____

_____

_____

_____

_____

_____

_____

The Kernel Journal - *Attitude*

How can you improve control over your attitude?

_____

_____

_____

_____

_____

_____

_____

_____

_____

_____

_____

_____

_____

_____

_____

_____

_____

_____

_____

_____

_____

_____

_____

Perseverance

"The powerful lesson of my ancestor burns deeply within my large heart," says the Ant reverently.

"Large heart," chuckles the Businessman. "It can't be bigger than a pinpoint."

"I speak in terms of courage, bravery, compassion, commitment, dedication, loyalty and perseverance" retorts the Ant curtly. "I dare you to match your heart against these qualifiers."

"I apologize," the Businessman says humbly seeking forgiveness.

"My ancestor teaches a great lesson of perseverance when seventy times he tries before moving a single kernel of corn over a wall to feed and supply his colony. Without this perseverance the colony is left hungry and wanting. Instilled in each of us is a relentless perseverance to never stop working. Is this apparent as you observe my colony," submits the Ant?

"This is very obvious," the Businessman responds looking at the never ending activity of the ant colony.

"This quality is an outgrowth of all the qualities we're discussing," teaches the Ant. "Living all these qualities brings with them the quality of perseverance. This is the synergy of the colony. That's a word I hear often in your circles, 'synergy'. When the culmination of all qualities together is greater than the individual characteristics, you're creating synergy. The resolve we have combined with the principles we live brings greater success to our colony than any of the individual values added together. Millenniums of progress teaches us perseverance is readily obtained through living the principles of which we speak."

"Perseverance keeps us going even when it is difficult. Perseverance keeps us going against overwhelming odds. Perseverance keeps us going through impossible situations. With perseverance, we work with devotion. Through perseverance we own the fruits of our work. Every ant in our colony learns this lesson; greatness always perseveres."

The Kernel Journal - *Perseverance*

What requires your perseverance?

_____

_____

_____

_____

_____

_____

_____

_____

_____

_____

_____

_____

_____

_____

_____

_____

_____

_____

_____

_____

_____

_____

The Kernel Journal - *Perseverance*

What do you need to give up to have stronger persever-ance?

_____

_____

_____

_____

_____

_____

_____

_____

_____

_____

_____

_____

_____

_____

_____

_____

_____

_____

_____

_____

_____

_____

Communicating Change

"Do you know how we communicate," the Ant asks the Businessman?

"I suppose there is more than just speaking 'ant,'" is the response.

"Right you are. Most communication comes through touch," the ant proclaims.

"I will be out of business in a day if there is

touching in our company," is the Businessman's animated reply. "This principle is not applicable to my company."

"Ever tire of being wrong," the Ant asks, sarcastically.

"I am not wrong," is the quick reply.

"If I agree with you we will both be wrong," says the Ant, smugly. "Let me explain. Our communication is touch. Our antenna contact tells us where we're going, where we are working, and what roles we play. This is the way we work together. "

Communication passes in our community with lighting speed. Without clear, concise, and immediate communication lines the ant colony will die."

"Communication," sighs the Businessman. "The biggest challenge of all."

"I share some imperatives," responds the Ant. "Speed, accuracy, simplicity; the proven principles of effective communication. We are built different than you. We communicate through different means. Your communication tools are very different. You have capability beyond your physical makeup. We rely solely on touch."

"Although seemingly primitive, this method accentuates principles honed and proven from the beginning of time. This is how we communicate. This is how we survive. This is how we thrive."

"Your technology is obsolete unless it enhances the principles of speed, accuracy, and simplicity. Adherence to these values brings effective communication. Here is a valuable lesson; Effective communication brings greatness."

The Kernel Journal - *Communicating Change*

What message does your communication style send?

_____

_____

_____

_____

_____

_____

_____

How can you better communicate your feelings and emotions?

_____

_____

_____

_____

_____

_____

_____

The Kernel Journal - *Communicating Change*

How well do you understand the emotions of others communicating to you?

_____

_____

_____

_____

_____

_____

_____

_____

_____

_____

_____

_____

_____

_____

_____

_____

_____

_____

_____

_____

Heritage

"I take you back to my ancestor who heroically moves the kernel of corn weighing many times more than his own weight over the wall. Seventy times it takes him, but he succeeds," proudly states the Ant.

"A very impressive heritage, you must be proud," submits the Businessman.

"Very proud," is the Ant's response. "The heritage of those who go before us helps us see who we are and who we can become."

"My heritage affects my success," the Businessman questions?

"Absolutely," is the Ant's reply.

"I am surprised. I feel I make my own success. I'm not dependent upon my ancestors," the Businessman confidently states.

"Certainly your dependence isn't upon your ancestors," teaches the Ant, "but you are leaving out a most important part of success if you don't access the best of your past. Let me explain with some questions. Where did you get your wavy hair? Where did you get the dimple in your chin? Where did you get the color of your eyes?"

The Businessman thinks for a moment, "I got my wavy hair from my mother, my dimple from my great-grandfather, and my blue eyes from my dad."

"Very good," the Ant nods. "And how do you know this?"

"I have family pictures. I hear family stories. I

talk with relatives," expresses the Businessman.

"Very good," compliments the Ant. "Now, your gift of diligence, your gift of punctuality, your gift for financial insight, where are these from?

"These are mine," says the Businessman indignantly.

"You are wrong," scolds the Ant. "You develop and nurture these characteristics, but they come to you from your heritage. When you realize this, you appreciate more fully these gifts given from your ancestors. You recognize the timeless values instilled in you come from generations before. You yearn to magnify these unique qualities to honor past generations. Your success passes the torch of excellence into the future. This is an important lesson for the Ant. Like Ants, you are the product of great qualities passed on for generations. Learn, appreciate, expand, perfect, and then teach others. This is the pattern of meaningful success. This is the pattern of continuing and lasting success. This is the success that leads to greatness."

The Kernel Journal - *Heritage*

What can you learn from your heritage?

_____

_____

_____

_____

_____

_____

_____

What can you appreciate?

_____

_____

_____

_____

_____

_____

_____

The Kernel Journal - *Heritage*

What can you expand?

_____

_____

_____

_____

_____

_____

_____

_____

What can you perfect?

_____

_____

_____

_____

_____

_____

_____

_____

The Kernel Journal - *Heritage*

How can you teach others?

_____
_____
_____
_____
_____
_____
_____
_____

How strong is the legacy you are building?

_____
_____
_____
_____
_____
_____
_____
_____

Farewell

"My talents are needed in the colony," states the Ant.

"I am thankful for your time," the Businessman says to the little creature. "You've taught a seemingly important businessman much about success."

"Less about success and more about greatness," is the Ant's response.

"Success comes and goes. Many corporations at the pinnacle of success fall quickly into decline and irrelevance. Success is seldom permanent. Success is often fleeting. This is the difference between success and greatness."

"Greatness lasts. Greatness isn't measured on financial gains and stock market accomplishments. All the wealth in the world can't overshadow the greatness of a single ant colony."

"Ant colonies flourish because each ant has a place and responsibility. Ant colonies build their culture on timeless and proven principles. Ant colonies thrive because their culture is refined and perfected. The culture created from these principles lives in every ant."

"And the principles of the ant colony are principles of greatness," surmises the Businessman.

"You are a quick learner," the Ant congratulates the Businessman.

"As you leave, I will share with you a saying you have heard differently over the years. It originates with a man in the 13th Century watching my ancestor lift a kernel seventy times before cresting the wall. Impressed with this feat, the man says to himself, 'Wise men learn through experience. Wiser men learn through the experience of the ant.'"

With that sound advice the Ant takes his place among the swarming colony and the solitary Businessman slowly jogs away toward greatness.

www.ingramcontent.com/pod-product-compliance
Lightning Source LLC
Chambersburg PA
CBHW020508100426
42813CB00030B/3162/J